To all the animals we've lost
before we ever knew to miss them—
especially small, quiet things like
snails and moths and little black birds
TP

To my dad and Nicole,
for introducing me to the Island,
and to all travelers who arrive bravely
on wind, on wings, on waves—may
we care for one another
MJ

First edition 2024. Library of Congress Catalog Card Number pending. ISBN 978-1-5362-1949-4. This book was typeset in Sweater School and Palatino. The illustrations were created digitally using handmade textures.
Candlewick Press, 99 Dover Street, Somerville, Massachusetts 02144. www.candlewick.com.
Printed in Humen, Dongguan, China. 24 25 26 27 28 29 APS 10 9 8 7 6 5 4 3 2 1

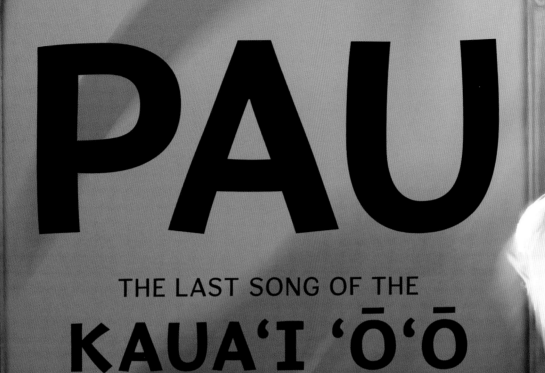

# PAU

## THE LAST SONG OF THE
## KAUA'I 'Ō'Ō

**Tony Piedra
& Mackenzie Joy**

CANDLEWICK PRESS

A long, long time ago,
an Island was born.
Over millions of years,
plants and animals
arrived . . .

5.1 MILLION YEARS AGO

on wind,
on wings,
and on waves.

From one of these travelers,
the 'ō'ō were born.

2 MILLION YEARS AGO

And for hundreds of thousands of years,
their song filled the Island.

Then a few people came to the Island.

400–1000 CE

The people brought a little—
a few new plants,
a few new animals.
They built a few shelters,
and they built a few gardens.

1000–1200 CE

The 'ō'ō moved—
away from the gardens,
from the shelters,
from the people.
But still there were many 'ō'ō,
and their song filled the Island.

1200–1777 CE

JANUARY 1778 CE

Then more people came to the Island.

They brought more and
they built more.

1778–1830 CE

More people, plants, and animals.

1830–1920 CE

More buildings, roads, and towns.

1920–1960 CE

More and more meant less and less.
Less room for the ʻōʻō.
Less of their song filled the Island.

Kauaʻi ʻōʻō

PAU?

MISSING

REWARD

LOST PET

PLEASE HELP

1960–1966 CE

A few people wondered,
where had the 'ō'ō gone?

The people followed their song.

They watched,
    and listened,
        and counted.

Then came a storm.
It battered the Island
with lightning and thunder,
wind, and rain.

NOVEMBER 1982 CE

After the storm,
the people rebuilt the towns.
They rebuilt the buildings.

But they couldn't rebuild the 'ō'ō.

*Were there any 'ō'ō left?*

They watched,
    and listened,
        and counted.

AUGUST 6, 1984 CE

They found only one.

One ʻōʻō left on the Island.

One ʻōʻō left in the world, still singing.

1985—1987 CE

1987 CE—PRESENT DAY

And then it was gone.

Pau.

# What does it mean that the Kaua'i 'ō'ō is pau?

Kaua'i 'ō'ō

PAU?

This book tells the story of the Kaua'i 'ō'ō, a Hawaiian forest bird that evolved and flourished for hundreds of thousands of years, then declined, then disappeared forever only a few decades ago. The Hawaiian word pau means finished, ended, or all done.

Extinction is not new. You probably already know about the dinosaurs going extinct around sixty-six million years ago. But did you know that right now, more species than ever before—plants and animals around our planet—are endangered or disappearing? The main difference between the time when the dinosaurs went extinct and the present is us: humans, and our measurable impact on the earth.

And yet humans have the capacity to learn and to change. The scientists who observed, documented, and recorded the extinction of the Kaua'i 'ō'ō learned more than just facts about its life—more than its wingspan, its diet, its mating habits. They discovered some of the whys. Why this forest bird vanished. And why the remaining forest birds of Kaua'i are vanishing. What the scientists learned is changing the way we live on this planet and is teaching us how to protect and save the species we have left. What they learned can encourage the rest of us to observe, listen, and learn, too. It's hard work, but it is important.

As of 2023, the remaining eight endemic forest bird species of Kaua'i are still disappearing. The main cause for this continued decline is avian malaria, transmitted by non-native mosquitoes. One such bird being affected is the 'akikiki. There are an estimated forty 'akikiki left on the island. An organization called the Kaua'i Forest Bird Recovery Project is working to preserve the 'akikiki. Whether there is enough time to save them is unknown. There is time, however, to promote knowledge and appreciation, preservation and conservation, so that future generations will know that the 'akikiki and the Kaua'i 'ō'ō were here once upon a time.

An increase in one species will often mean a decrease in another, but by observing, we can remember. By remembering, we can learn. By learning, we can change. We can change the nature of our impact.

## Can you spot these birds and other animals of Kaua'i?

### ENDEMIC (NATIVE) SPECIES

1. 'akikiki, or Kaua'i creeper (*Oreomystis bairdi*): endemic to Kaua'i; critically endangered

2. Kaua'i 'ō'ō (*Moho braccatus*): endemic to Kaua'i: extinct

3. nēnē, or Hawaiian goose (*Branta sandvicensis*): endemic to the Hawaiian islands; formerly critically endangered, now near threatened

### SPECIES INTRODUCED BY POLYNESIANS

4. 'īlio, 'īlio māku'e, or Hawaiian poi dog (*Canis familiaris*): extinct breed

5. moa, or red junglefowl (*Gallus gallus*)

6. Polynesian rat (*Rattus exulans*)

7. pua'a, or feral pig (*Sus scrofa*)

### SPECIES INTRODUCED BY EUROPEANS

8. black rat (*Rattus rattus*)

9. feral cat (*Felis catus*)

10. mosquito (*Culex quinquefasciatus*)

11. zebra dove (*Geopelia striata*)

# A Brief History of the Kaua'i 'ō'ō

**5.1 million years ago** • The island of Kaua'i forms in the Pacific Ocean from volcanic activity and is slowly populated by plants and animals. Scientists estimate that one new species arrived every 10,000 to 100,000 years.

**2 million years ago\*** • A species of waxwing arrives and evolves into the Kaua'i 'ō'ō, a forest bird. In total, fifty-seven species of forest birds, collectively known as honeycreepers, evolve on the Hawaiian islands and are found nowhere else in the world.

**400–1000 CE\*** • The first humans arrive on the island. These Polynesian travelers from the Marquesas Islands are highly skilled seafarers, farmers, and fishers.

**1000–1200** • The travelers introduce twenty-seven new species of plants (known as canoe plants) and a few new animals: pua'a (pigs), moa (chickens), and 'ilio (dogs), as well as, unintentionally, rats, which hitch rides as stowaways.

**1200–1777** • Lowland forests are clear-cut for farming. The Kaua'i 'ō'ō adapts by moving inland and up into the mountain forests, which are unsettled.

**January 1778** • Captain James Cook of England lands his two ships, *Resolution* and *Discover*, at the island. They are the first-known Europeans to reach Hawai'i.

**1778–1830** • Europeans further clear-cut the island, leading to more habitat loss. They also bring new plants and animals, some of which become invasive. One of the smallest, and ultimately the most damaging, invasive species is the mosquito, introduced in 1826.

**1830–1920** • Sugarcane becomes Kaua'i's dominant industry, and people travel from all over the world to work on the island's plantations. Many indigenous and endemic species go extinct, but the Kaua'i 'ō'ō is still commonly seen and heard as late as 1890.

**1920–1960** • The tourism industry develops. The first cases of avian malaria and avian pox, spread by mosquitos, are detected in 1940. The Kaua'i 'ō'ō are now considered rare and are even twice thought to have gone extinct, once in the 1940s and again in the 1950s.

**1960–1966** • Tourism surges, and the impacts on the Kaua'i 'ō'ō and other indigenous and endemic species compound. The Kaua'i 'ō'ō has an estimated population of about thirty-six individuals left.

**1967–1981** • Field biologist John Sincock arrives in Kaua'i to study Hawaiian species. He partners with local scientists, historians, knowledge keepers, and others to learn and design an approach for observing and counting endangered Hawaiian bird species.

*'Ōhi'a lehua*
*(Metrosideros polymorpha)*

 **November 1982** • Hurricane Iwa makes landfall on November 19–23, damaging or destroying more than two thousand buildings and thousands of acres of habitat, leaving humans and other animals without homes. US biologists head into the Alaka'i Swamp, the most pristine forest left on the island, to see if the last two known Kaua'i 'ō'ō survived the storm. They observe only one male.

 **August 6, 1984** • On a sighting expedition, scientists hear a Kaua'i 'ō'ō's song; they take out a tape recorder and begin to record. After the bird flits away, they rewind and play the tape of the song. As the humans listen to the recorded song, the original bird flies back and sings. The last Kaua'i 'ō'ō on earth is singing to itself.

 **1985–1987** • The final Kaua'i 'ō'ō is observed going through nest-building rituals and calling over and over for a mate. The bird is officially last heard on April 29, 1987.

 **1987–present day** • Continued efforts to find Kaua'i 'ō'ō are unsuccessful. In 1992, Hurricane Iniki wreaks fresh devastation on the island. In 2021, the US Fish and Wildlife Service declares the Kaua'i 'ō'ō extinct, along with three other Kaua'i bird species, and ceases efforts to locate it.

*Estimate only; scientists and researchers concede that greater precision is challenging to achieve.

## Selected Bibliography

Denny, Jim. *The Birds of Kaua'i*. Honolulu: University of Hawai'i Press, 1999.

Lewis, Daniel. *Belonging on an Island: Birds, Extinction, and Evolution in Hawai'i*. New Haven: Yale University Press, 2018.

Pratt, H. Douglas. *A Pocket Guide to Hawai'i's Trees and Shrubs*. Honolulu: Mutual Publishing, 2004.

Walther, Michael, illustrated by Julian P. Hume. *Extinct Birds of Hawai'i*. Honolulu: Mutual Publishing, 2016.

Tony Piedra learned about the Kaua'i 'ō'ō when he saw the 2015 documentary *Racing Extinction*, directed by Louie Psihoyos, which explores the urgent race to protect species from threats of extinction, https://www.opsociety.org/our-work/films/racing-extinction/.

Mackenzie Joy learned about the Kaua'i 'ō'ō when she listened to John Green's podcast, *The Anthropocene Reviewed*, episode 20: "QWERTY Keyboard Kaua'i 'ō'ō," September 26, 2019, https://www.wnycstudios.org/podcasts/anthropocene-reviewed/episodes/anthropocene-reviewed-qwerty-keyboard-and-kauai-o-o.

## For Further Exploration

**Cornell Lab of Ornithology: Birds of the World**
https://birdsoftheworld.org/bow/home

**Cornell Lab of Ornithology: Macaulay Library**
Last verified recording of the Kaua'i 'ō'ō, May 1986, Jim Jacobi
https://macaulaylibrary.org/asset/228099

**Kaua'i Forest Bird Recovery Project**
https://kauaiforestbirds.org
This site provides more information on the bird species pictured on the endpapers of this book. And check out the video "Songbird: a virtual moment of extinction in Hawaii," https://kauaiforestbirds.org/kauai-forest-bird-360-virtual-reality-educational-educational-video/.

Scan the QR code to listen to an original field recording of the Kaua'i 'ō'ō: